PARENT POWER

*Parent Power Workbook - A Guide and Workbook
for the journey of being a Single Parent*

ZANDRA J. DEOROSAN

WESTBOW
PRESS®
A DIVISION OF THOMAS NELSON
& ZONDERVAN

WestBow Press books may be ordered through booksellers or by contacting:

WestBow Press
A Division of Thomas Nelson & Zondervan
1663 Liberty Drive
Bloomington, IN 47403
www.westbowpress.com
844-714-3454

ISBN: 978-1-6642-4065-0 (sc)
ISBN: 978-1-6642-4064-3 (e)

Print information available on the last page.

WestBow Press rev. date: 07/27/2021

Parent Power Preface

Parents and Families today in 2020, are not traditionally defined. <u>The traditional family that consists of two parents with 2.5 kids has changed immensely.</u> There are families that have grandparents raising children. There are families that have single dads raising children. And then there are single mothers raising children. With single mothers raising children being a staple in families today, the percentage is greater than both single dads and grandparents combined. However, according to a US Census Bureau Report from 2016, 23 million families living arrangements are that of single parents, of which mothers, head the household. (Nov,2016)

The parents and families of today need help. They need support. They need POWER! To effectively function and raise a family in today's climate of technology and social media headliners, a parent can get lost, overwhelmed, even depressed! I raised my children as a single parent! And I understand the plight, the quandary, the tight situations, and the hopelessness! AND through THE GRACE OF GOD, I MADE IT!!

I write to this book with the hopes of bringing inspiration, motivation, help and happiness to THE SINGLE PARENT!

In the Beginning

I married at 26, with hopes of having a big family, much like my parents. Our family consisted of 12 people, ten children and two parents. This huge family back in the day was fine at the time. The world was different then and although there were many family types, large two-parent (mother, father) families as the one I was born into and grew with was the most common, it was normal. The thing that most young men and women aspired to do, be a husband or a wife, have a big family. But just as this family type was common from one house to the next, growing up with all these people in one household was really challenging because you fight and long for your place in the family as well as search for attention. Oddly, enough my parents had the intense energy to pay attention to every kid, all of the time. All five boys and all five girls. They would remember and know all our names by heart and even by personality or the child-like behavior every child possesses.

<u>When I had my first child, I was expecting to endure the long-lasting rocky marriage relationship like my parents and continue to have children before finally finding my way between wife and motherhood.</u> Just like my parents did. My husband and I loved one another and worked together for the most part. Our days were somewhat pleasurable, and I handled the transition from being a single, independent female sharing an apartment with her sister to an instant bride and new mother well. The challenges and obstacles of us learning our family and friends as well as each other was easy for me and easy for him. So, we both adjusted fine. Our lives quickly changed though, when my husband lost his job working as an Armed Security Transport Guard. He became hopeless and quiet. As much as I tried to help in the situation, it seemed to grow worse, and I had just given birth to our first child, Ayanna, a baby girl. The days turned to weeks with no responses from employers for my husband.

However, my marriage happened to be long-lasting in feeling and short lived on happiness. Although I loved my husband, our rockiness was getting harder and harder for me to deal with as time marched on. By the birth of our second child, my husband lost his job and me pregnant and limited income, I began to think about what happened to my parents when the split between them occurred. It was also about not having enough income to "feed the family".

So, I began to weather the storms and move through our challenges with GOD helping me each time I asked, and every time I prayed. At the birth of my third child, the decision to divorce came swiftly to my mind when I woke up one day. It just hit me that one morning, early. I stumbled from bed all big and pregnant, waddled to the restroom and the thought kept coming. Almost like a bad headache. On this day at that time, I was immediately rock solid over the marriage and with having children, everything family, everything wife all of it. But, I was also not happy with the notion of being a single parent either. The notion of having to handle all of the two-parent responsibilities by myself. No one to rely on or talk to and discuss things with. I was just not ready for it. Nope! Nope! Nope!

The separation came before the divorce and that was hardest to deal with, seeing my husband leave our home, then seeing him again before the divorce papers were signed. I felt weird, different and in despair when the separation happened. Although each day I woke up became easier to manage, the moments of realizing that I was not a married person anymore kinda' devastated me. I compared this to when my parents "divorced", "separated" or whatever they called it then. And even though we (my brothers and sisters) did not sit before a judge inside a divorce court, talk to a divorce lawyer or some type of social worker, devastation happened then, and it was happening to ME now!

The transition from wife and mother...to mother, father, caregiver, provider, nurturer, disciplinarian, teacher, and all other hats that come with being a single parent was thrust upon ME... My wife and mother title now became Mother and then SOME!!! I was a single parent mother with two children and a newborn.

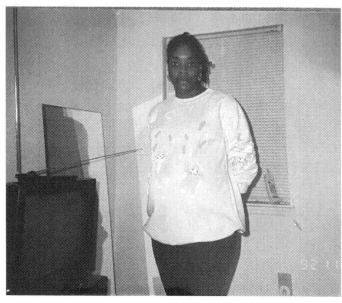

Zandra, pregnant

HELP?

Before the divorce, me, my kids (Alex and Ayanna) and my husband were living in a two-and-a-half-bathroom apartment. The neighborhood where the apartment was located was on a street named, "Favor" Road. This road was not favorable to me, but it was a place to live, and our home. Our apartment complex was not well kept but decent and somewhat clean. The managers and maintenance crews responsible for keeping the complex together did an ok job but quickly harassed a tenant for monies when monthly rent payments were not paid on time. It was pretty much an income/low income-based apartment complex with many families and small children residing everywhere. My husband located this place while we were in transition from his truck driving position. We traveled over-the-road for nearly 1 year, before realizing that a family needs a stable place to live. One of my husband's co-workers let him know about this "horrible" apartment complex but we both knew it was affordable. I decided to be thankful rather than grumpy and look at the truck again. So with everything in me I did just that. The place was not appealing but it was affordable.

My husband and I argued and disagreed regularly about everything from money to sex. And we tried the best way possible to get along with each other but we both saw no future past the point where we stood. The long unbearable road trip living within a huge eighteen-wheeler truck with a small bed, no refrigerator or place to walk was wild and the trip took a huge toll on our married life. There was a time when we sought out counseling from a Christian Counseling Service because we both felt like this would help us communicate and see some form of hope in our marriage, in our lives together. After about two weeks of meeting once a week, it just didn't work. The therapist would let me know that, the sessions required both parties to be involved. My husband just would not show up. Since I had more sessions to go anyway, the therapist and I decided it would help me to attend one last time, then cancel the remaining sessions. We both tried to stop the separation from happening, but it was not avoidable.

No HELP!? Were the most dominating words in my mind, day after day when that new week came in and I had no scheduled session available… I began reaching out to anyone that would listen. My next door neighbor listened but her advice was subjective, so it didn't really matter. "Just forget him, feed him and send him to work", she'd say at the end of every conversation. So our talks were limited to "Hey, what's up…" Silence then, "OK thanks…Bye!" That's it. I needed something else. Shortly after I ended "the neighborly advice", I began attending a church. The church was a considerable drive from the apartment but I tried not to think about it, on Sundays and especially during the week on Wednesdays I attended. Of course my husband did not attend because he was conveniently unavailable for either day, so I went alone with Alex and Ayanna. After our first few visits, I began to feel better emotionally. It was as if the hope I had in myself was being restored. The hopelessness was fading. Not leaving, just fading. There's a big difference. My kids loved the place. They fed them dinner some nights when we were there and kept them for a few minutes longer if I decided to stay and listen to the choir singing after the sermons were preached. This church also helped my kids feel good like kids should feel, happy, alive, fun and full of life! This was good for them, real good. This was good for me because I needed to "soak" up all the inspiration my body could hold to make it back home again and keep going. People don't realize the power and the essential need for inspiration. It's like food and water. Power is the Food that gives you energy and keep you going, Water is the Essential that quenches your thirst. I think this may have been the "something else" I was looking for in my neighbor but just could not describe it. I also realized that No HELP!? Hadn't left but it was fading, little by little, it was fading.

After making it back to our apartment one night, I washed up Alex and Ayanna quickly then put them to bed. Although

I felt better and began to experience the hopelessness fading, I felt nauseated. At first thought, it was something I ate from earlier in the day, but as I walked around the room, the nausea grew. Then all of a sudden I ran to the bathroom, and THREW UP! Ugghhh!! I hope not!! Please let this be food poisoning or some expired meat. I quickly walked over to the medicine cabinet where I kept bandages, Vaseline, sunscreen, lotions that type of thing. I located a pregnancy test that I picked up from the pharmacy one day prior to this day. It was new enough to be used, so I went through the instructions and waited for the 30 minute test period to be completed. *"God please let this feeling of sickness be something other than pregnancy. I can't be pregnant, I must not be pregnant, I don't WANT to be pregnant!! AGAIN!!!"* After washing the dishes in the kitchen sink, I walked slowly back to the bathroom, just hoping for a negative test result. There the sample was on the bathroom sink ready for me to check.

At first I checked the sample using the night light in the plug next to the sink. *"It was negative"* I sighed! Fell to the floor and began thanking GOD that I was NOT pregnant and went about my business of getting ready for bed. But, as I looked at the sample closer, it changed color from the light pink under the night light, to a darker pink. I flipped the bathroom light switch. *"Ughhhhh!" I screamed,* for at least ten minutes. Then I cried for fifteen minutes. As I cried, I felt the pain of challenges and struggles ahead. My mind racing terribly. Another child? Really? Not another child! Alex and Ayanna were enough for me to handle. The pain

was present, the pain was real. Hopelessness returned. I
needed inspiration again before bed. I fell asleep.

I woke up in the morning to find that my husband moved
out. Here I was pregnant with our third child and without a
full-time income. I prayed for a miracle to happen. I worried
too about money among other things, we could be evicted.
While my soon-to-be ex-husband paid me small payments,
it still was not enough to pay the rent and utilities in our tiny
two-bedroom apartment. I decided to look for other ways
of getting income, so I went to the Department of Family
and Children Services (DFCS). They offered financial
support in the amount of a small monthly payment, medical
assistance for each of us and food support otherwise known
as Food Stamps.

As I continued to look for help and assistance, I tried to
stay encouraged for an answer to come. Later, me and my
two kids drove to a nearby park. As I watched my daughter
Ayanna and son Alexander play in the sand box and swing
on the monkey bars at the park's playground, I heard a voice
from inside of myself. The voice was peaceful, yet strong,
quiet yet firm. It said, "I will provide for you." When I first
heard this voice, I thought I was daydreaming, or hearing
another person speak to me. So, I began to look around,
only to notice Ayanna and Alex running around at the park
and playing with each other. I walked over to a bench away
from the sand box area and sat down. This time, the voice
grew stronger than it had been before. "I will provide for
you." I knew this was not me, nor another person standing

or sitting next to me. It was GOD. By now, the kids and myself had been at the park for an hour. I watched them as they continued to play, I stood up from the bench and began walking around the track near the playground. The first lap I walked around left me thirsty and out of breath. I was about a month and a half pregnant now. My doctor thought I was further along given the pregnancy test date from a recent appointment. *"I wondered about that date also. I was probably pregnant long before the test".* My doctor also thought that I would deliver early so, she suggested I walk a little more to help with giving birth, which was another reason for being at the park. I walked over to our car and grabbed a few bottles of water. Alex and Ayanna came running down to get them and then quickly ran back to the playground. On my second lap I heard the same voice again, for a third time "I will provide for you." After we arrived back at our apartment, I could see a note taped to the door coming into view as we drove up. The closer I drove into the parking lot, I could easily notice that it was from our apartment leasing office, they left a note on my door. Ayanna grabbed the note and brought it inside with us, where she set it on the table. A few minutes later, I sat at the table and read it and the others as well.

The lease office notice stated that I had 30 days (about 4 and a half weeks) to exit the apartment, or I would be forced out from the local police or sheriff's department.

Zandra and kids

No POWER!

At my doctor's beautiful, plush, office, I looked around at the other women waiting. One woman was on the telephone speaking to her husband; another woman was waiting to see our obstetrician/ gynecologist; another woman's husband checked her in at the front desk while she located a place to sit. This huge, strange feeling nearly blanketed my body, and I began to feel powerless!

I almost felt like I was having a mental breakdown of some sort. Like these women had their husbands with them, (Where was mine!). The power to have a supportive husband whose assistance and words of encouragement was so very much needed! Escaped me! It was not there for me as I witnessed with these women.

The overwhelming feeling of powerlessness had me holding back tears as I stared around the room. After making my way into the examination room I laid my big round body on the exam table bed thingy and watched the monitor during my ultrasound. The technician commented on the baby's size, weight, and overall appearance like they do in the ninth month of pregnancy. I was not nervous. I was powerless. I was not scared. I was powerless. I was not worried. I WAS POWERLESS!! The definition of powerless as defined by the Merriam-Webster's Dictionary says this, "devoid of strength or resources." And that is just one definition! But today at this moment, I felt powerless, left without strength or resources. The women I just mentioned, could have felt powerless in their lives at some point, I am so sure. But not at that time, their time of need and support; their time of assistance and encouragement. They were not like me; they were not POWERLESS.

The technician finished the scanning and next, my wonderful doctor walked in. I could not have prayed for a sweeter person to be my obstetrician/gynecologist. Dr. Anderson had amazing bed side manners and treated every patient as if it were her first. She was concerned about me as a woman, a mother and as her patient. In that order. During most of my visits we spent at least 20 minutes talking about my psychological and mental health. I found Dr. Anderson after a grueling search of doctors. It took a week of me visiting and being examined from six to eight different doctors within the practice at the

Atlanta Gynecologist/Obstetrician Group in hopes of narrowing down which person would be my choice for a practicing physician going forward. After the normal formalities of the visit finished, she immediately went into discussing the birth of the baby and all the hospital procedures for the day of and after of the baby's delivery. As she spoke, I felt the feeling of powerlessness come over me as it had done before and as this happened, I was thinking "I had no one to check me in to the hospital for delivery day, no one to be in the delivery room at the time my precious baby was being born" No Help! No POWER! But then, suddenly, a voice quiet, still, small, inside of me as I knew it was, over shadowed Dr. Anderson's voice. It overshadowed my own thinking inside of my mind, so much that I only heard THIS voice while looking attentively and actively moving my eyes around and upon Dr. Anderson. All I could hear was, "I WILL PROVIDE FOR YOU!! The doctor wished me well and said, "I will see you next week."

HIM?

By now, as you are reading this book and I hope you get the picture. My husband moved out; I AM a single parent. I must do it all! See to my children's needs, (school, home, emotional, physical), demands of work, pregnancy, and my own self-worth. There is no HIM? A partner to assist, a partner to support, a partner to encourage. I did not have HIM? But I needed HIM, (him? was my husband). The workday was rough, by the time I saw Alex and Ayanna, I was exhausted. They were glad to see me, happy to know that I was there for them. The baby girl in my stomach seemed excited as well. She moved, she kicked and turned over and over. This feeling was so soothing, so beautiful, carrying another human being inside of my body is such a gift. I knew it. I cherished it. I did not take it for granted.

In the car, we were headed to church. I had to get to another place in my mind because the feeling of powerlessness stayed with me. The music was loud and inspirational, the singers' voices pierced my heart in a wonderful way. After dropping my children off into the "children's church," I walked into the huge sanctuary and down its corridor isle of blue carpet and clothed covered chairs. I quickly found a seat, (where the ushers seated me) and threw my belongings down in the chair next to me and immediately began my praise and worship experience. From one song to the next, I listened, I sang along, I meditated and then did it all over again. Worship. It drowned out my thoughts, it drowned out the challenges, it drowned out the fear and it drowned out the powerlessness. I found HIM? (HIM? My husband? Nah! GOD! That's who!) I found HIM!

Delivery!!

D r. Anderson arrived on time; I was ready, ready. To deliver my precious baby girl! The pain was unbearable. The feeling of powerlessness came again. This time, it was much stronger than when I first experienced it. The team of medicals gathered all the tools and equipment, put them in place and here she came!

I pushed one time, as Dr. Anderson instructed me. She didn't scream or yell for me to push, she simply just said, "Now get ready and push." After the first break from the second push, I felt different. The childbirth pain did not disappear, but the amount of pain diminished. As I looked toward the ceiling, I heard God say, "I AM WITH YOU" and then a warm sensation covered me. Almost like a blanket wrapping me up. Dr. Anderson gave me a final instruction and out she came! The most beautiful and sweetest little girl, ever! She cried, I cried, we ALL cried.

The hospital was wonderful for new mothers (again). I stayed for two days. On the third day, I went back to my apartment. Alex and Ayanna had to meet their new little sister. My apartment neighbor stayed with them while I was at the hospital. She was great. Smoked cigarettes a lot, but she was great and my two did will with her. The energy of feeling brand new again rushed me and I enjoyed having all my kids by me, near me. My husband visited shortly after I returned to the apartment.

It turned out to be a full day, with having a newborn baby and then adjusting to taking care of two others (children) all at once. I immediately felt the pressure of being a mother, disciplining as though I were the father, then bursting into song and dance wearing a host of other hats (chef, nurse…) in the short, quick 24 hours. My children were finally asleep, including the newborn. I laid on the sofa and could not help but cry. Cry for myself, cry for my children, cry about the challenges that I have yet to face. But then here comes the voice of GOD, which I began to know and understand that that's just what it was. "I Am With You" His voice stated. Repeatedly, at least three times, maybe more, in my crying I couldn't keep a count. I delivered a new human being, only now I realized, that I too needed a Delivery!

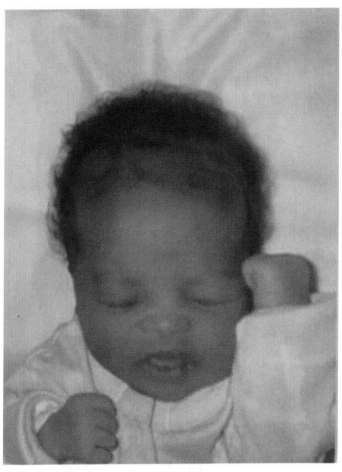

Angela as a baby

"I Win!"

Out with the OLD and
In with the NEW

A month later the notice of eviction came taped to my apartment door. The phone rang and it was the attorney's office that I contacted about filing for divorce. The attorney and I discussed the process, the paperwork, and the fees. While he answered many questions about dissolving a marriage by divorce (this was my first marriage), the money issues to get this process and paperwork started was my concern. My thoughts immediately became negative, overwhelming, frustrating, and weak. But the warm sensation I felt in the hospital came over my me again as I heard the same voice of God say, "I Am With YOU." After we finished speaking, I looked at the furniture notice. The notice stated the company would be coming to pick up my furniture for non-payment. They were coming soon, like that day, at that moment! I quickly gathered my kids and left for the park playground again. It seemed as if the park was a peaceful place for both me and my kids. I left the apartment right away. So, I figured, if I'm not at the apartment when they arrive, then they can't take my furniture. As I drove, I kept hearing the voice of God say to me "I AM With YOU" all the way to the park.

We stopped to grab food from McDonald's just before going on into the playground parking lot. As my kids sat and ate, I walked around the track with baby Angela inside a black stroller. At that moment, a telephone call came in. It was another attorney's office from the Atlanta Legal Aid Society. I had called them a month before I delivered Angela and it took a month like the receptionist stated, for them to phone me back. I was surprised and hopeful, but I could feel negativity and powerlessness began to dominate my thoughts. The receptionist asked several times if I had the money to retain a divorce attorney and the answer was still NO! I couldn't understand why she kept asking before she said, "Ma'am, people lie on the application and in person to receive our free legal services." "They provide lots of false information and we have to be sure." My mind was at ease a bit because I knew I was telling the truth. This was a real story on paper, in print. Not something I made up. As we continued to discuss my application and family situation, the receptionist said, "We can help you, but it may be a year."

My heart sank to the bottom of my stomach, I needed to be divorced right away. My marriage was not getting better and besides my husband was not in our apartment, he began to move ON…So I needed to do the same…The receptionist put me on hold for five minutes. The five minutes might as well have been five years. I prayed as this Hold, or Pause was happening, not sure of what to expect.

I needed help and I needed it now. After the receptionist came back on the line, she said, "Ms. Harrison (my married last name), I have an attorney for you, like right now not in a year!" I screamed "Hallelujah!" at the top of my lungs. My kids stopped playing on the playground and looked over at me. Baby Angela in the stroller moved around but stayed asleep. "Are you there?" she said. I gathered myself and returned to the call, she went on to say, that the attorney was a new attorney just out of law school and available in two days to meet. And the best part, no fee!

Whoa! That was awesome! I sang, I cried, I laughed, I danced right there where I was on the dusty, grimy, old, track. The powerlessness was leaving and leaving now!

"I Win!"

It Is Over!

Robin, the attorney was a true professional. He was careful and cautious. He discussed the entire process. He discussed the pros and the cons of what may happen in court. I felt relaxed and in control with Robin. He wanted to do the best for me and for my kids. I thanked God. The appointment was fast, and the next thing was to wait for the paperwork that my husband had to sign and the actual court appointment. Breathe In, Breathe Out! It's O-o-o-o-v-v-v-er-er....

Later, after the kids ate dinner, watched a few minutes of their favorite television program, bathed, and went to bed, I fumbled through the "divorce" paperwork. There it was 12-15 pages of words detailing my life for the last five years a marriage relationship type deal. I guess that's the only way I could describe it, anything else might not fit. The knock at the door was my soon-to-be ex-husband. It was not too late, around 8:00 p.m. I asked him to come over and sign the paperwork, he agreed. "Ok, so now what…," I thought walking to open the door.

We spoke briefly as he took a seat at the table. He looked angry or upset about something, could it be our breaking relationship, could it be someone new? I was not sure. The goal was to get the papers signed and returned to the attorney before the end of the week. I slid the neatly stapled, "Consent to Divorce" paperwork over to him. He lifted the top page, then the second page and went quickly to the last page. "So, what's all this mean…. irreconcilable differences… and irretrievably broken…and never to be reconciled again?" I was at a loss for words. "You know I could contest, this…" I was still at a loss for words, not knowing what to say to him? Robin, my attorney, said he may ask these questions or be reluctant to sign because "serving" divorce papers is like admitting failure or losing. I walked around the apartment in silence, pretending to not care. Like trying to be nonchalant about what was happening. Be relaxed and not anxious or worried or…. anything. I spoke a few words, waited, sighed, and kept my eyes on him. This moment could be so different right now and go in another direction. But then my husband embraced me quickly and let go. Here comes the feeling of powerlessness, all in a rush, quick and at that second! It was stronger like the first time! But here comes the voice of God! **Loud and strong**! Moving me past that powerlessness. Emotions!!! Amazing how my peace within me was just as loud and as strong, the same way as HIS VOICE!

After our embrace, the voice of God assured me, "I AM WITH YOU." I released a huge sigh. "I can contest this," my soon-to-be ex-husband stated again. Which made the think that *"contesting, the divorce was on his mind."* Instantly, I worried for the kids, knowing they could hear everything. I worried that he would try to take them away from me, like now. Right now. Then suddenly, we embraced, he quickly let me go, signed the papers, and walked out the door, slamming it behind him.

I fell to the floor thanking God with everything in me.

It's Over but not just YET!

There were three cases before mine, the court recording voicemail stated. I rushed around to get Alex and Ayanna to the daycare center. The center would not take care of Angela because she was too young and according to the daycare facility laws in Georgia, a child must be at least six to eight weeks old before receiving care from any childcare provider.

Angela was only one month old and a baby small in size. She looked much younger than that. I kept the time to the minute trying to drop them at the center and then make it for the divorce court at 8:00 am. The traffic on the highway was gridlocked, an accident! Downtown? I could remember Robin's voice at our last appointment, "Please be on time, the judge over your case is harsh. He doesn't like late court appearances and runs a strict courtroom." "And Oh! Another thing, he is a traditional-type judge who rarely grants divorces." So, by now, I am trying to not think about anything but get there, that's it. My little Angela was quietly sleeping as I sped through traffic and downtown Atlanta hoping to get a decent parking space near the courthouse. The traffic was horrible! I finally found a spot, grabbed Angela, and paid the fare.

Moments later as I enter the court room, I noticed a great many people who had cases at or around the same time, my goodness, the court was filled with people! There was Robin, he waved at me as I walked toward him. He noticed that Angela my baby was with me. "Why did you bring your baby daughter?" He asked. I knew I had no other choice at the time if I was going to make it here on time and GET the divorce! "I know, but I had no choice, she's not old enough to stay at a daycare center...and no one else was available." My voice started to crack, and I wanted to cry, but I held back the tears. Robin looked at me with uneasy eyes. He sighed and said, "OK, wait here." He disappeared into another room with one of the law clerks. I knew he was going to discuss my case before I was called. The sounds of the courtroom and people sitting in the squeaky wood "church pew" benches made me feel uneasy, but I had to go on. I could not reschedule for a new day, there was no time for another day! Today was the day! Robin returned with a better look on his face and I smiled a little. At least those few seconds were better than the last.

It was time for my case to be presented. The bailiff in his deep resonating voice stated, "All Rise, Judge W. Kramer, presiding." Everyone stood at attention, I worried that baby

Angela would begin to cry. She made a few noises and began to wake up so as soon as we all sat down, I grabbed her from the baby car seat I carried her in along with a bottle.

I watched Robin do his lawyer thing. He presented my case well, with honesty and good intentions. He was sharp and to the point. When he pointed me out to Judge Kramer, the judge asked me about Angela being in his courtroom. He went into how inappropriate it was to have a child of any age in his courtroom unless, it was extremely necessary. Robin reiterated my statement about the daycare issue to Judge Kramer, but he just kept looking at me. Angela was such a sweet baby and a good baby (she rarely cried or screamed out) that I hoped and prayed Judge Kramer would overlook the "inappropriateness." At one o'clock in the morning, the night before I was to appear in court, I prayed. After the encounter with my kid's dad, the feeling of powerlessness re-emerged. In rushing around to get all of us ready for the morning, I still felt it, but I pushed on to get to my new life. My new life as a single woman, but now, as a SINGLE mother! I was ready for the marriage to be over and ready to start again, but with so much responsibility of caring for children, myself....and so forth! I kept praying until I fell back asleep. "Mrs. Harrison why isn't your husband here today?" judge Kramer asked me. I already knew the answer. He didn't want to be. He was upset, mad, angry all at the same time. But I couldn't say that to the judge. And Robin, my attorney, he knew what I was thinking already just by looking at my face. "Um, your honor, he was unable to take time away from his job...and some other circumstances." I stated quickly. The judge was old, traditional, and staunch, just like Robin had said. At that moment, I heard GOD's voice say softly, peaceful, and still, "I AM WITH YOU."

The judge looked at me, he looked at Angela and continued. Robin was great! He really kept on top of the judge, his paperwork was in order and the legal clerk helped each time he requested. I sat back comfortably on the wooden benches rocking Angela a bit, keeping her consoled. We were almost finished! Next, Judge Kramer asked me about my living arrangements and plans for income.

I explained then Robin interjected. I thanked GOD for Robin! One last part, Judge Kramer to grant the divorce based on Robin's statements and written explanation's he read. The judge paused, I looked at Robin, he looked back at me, shrugged his shoulders, then back at Judge Kramer. Wow are you kidding me?! I said in my mind. What is this man (Kramer) thinking? He spoke, "Mrs. Harrison, I really don't like to grant a divorce for a couple without the couple first having marital counseling for at least four weeks. Then return to my courtroom and determine if divorce is necessary because there are children involved." I swallowed hard; my eyes were locked on Judge Kramer. "Are you kidding me! Counseling? there is no way..." The long pause after the judge spoke was about 3 seconds. Thankfully, Robin interjected and gave a complete explanation for the circumstances presented, again. As I cuddled Angela in my arms, and Robin finished speaking, the judge was silent once again. Then all at once I could see his hand go down to the paperwork in front of him. He was writing! He was signing! He was granting! "Divorce, GRANTED!!!" I sighed, looked to the ceiling and thanked GOD! My heart was light, Robin smiled and wiped his brow then I quickly gathered Angela, and my belongings and exited to the lobby. What a glorious day! What a freeing day! What a brand-new day!

"I Win!"

The New Chapter

A week later after the divorce was granted, Robin phoned to be certain me and my children were well. He also phoned to let me know that my divorce decree was in the mail. I thanked him for all his help. He was such a blessing to us! As I hung up the phone, I read the apartment notice again stating that we had to vacate the premises by the end of the week. It was Monday. What would happen? We needed a place to live. I had no money saved! I called the lease office to get clarification of the notice. The manager I spoke with explained and stated by Sunday evening of the week, my children and myself should be out of the apartment, if not other consequences would begin to occur. Although this was not good news for me, I remained upbeat, happy, and positive. I thanked GOD for a solution!

I began packing our belongings inside the apartment. I drove to a nearby grocery store and picked up a few empty boxes.

My car was loaded with them. On the way from the grocery store, I stopped at the mailbox center to grab my mail. It was just after 2:00 pm and the mail carrier finished his normal deliveries at our apartment building. The tiny letter sized; steel box was full of mail. I placed the rubber-band stack of mail inside my purse. Later that night after picking up Alex and Ayanna, bathing them and Angela, cooking and serving dinner, then finally getting time to myself, I sorted through the days mail. Lots of bills, junk mail, the usual stuff. I come across this last piece of mail addressed to me from the Housing Department of Marietta. This was not junk mail. As I open the letter, and quickly skim through the words, I gathered that my name was chosen to receive assistance with housing me and my children.

Wow! Wow! Wow! So excited, I rang from around the living room singing! I sang as loud as I could with the letter in my hand! I tip-toed up the stairs and kissed each kid, Alex, Angela and then Ayanna. I was so focused on getting the divorce from my husband, that I forgot about an earlier appointment with the Housing Department. I entered my name and address in a lottery-type system for parents and families needing assistance with housing. If the parent or family name were drawn, that family would receive a voucher to pay their monthly rent for as long as they remained with the program called Section 8.

Thank GOD! I got it! This was such a blessing! And at the right time! Wow! I ran back down stairs and fell to the floor, thanking GOD, for my solution had come!

At the end of the week, we moved into our new home! It was small, but just enough for US! The kids were excited! I was excited! Officially, me and my family crossed over into the new chapter, I walked in the front door, fell to the floor and Thanked GOD!

Alex, Ayanna, and Angela as adults

Parent Power: A Workbook for Self-Discovery as a Single Parent

This short workbook is designed to help a single parent rediscover themselves through the parenting process and maintain their purpose, passion self-worth along the way.

Knowing your personality helps in determining who you are as a person. I created this workbook on scribbled pieces of paper, to help guide me in my journey as a single parent. I read many articles that discussed the "Big 5 Personality Traits", which really began to open my heart and mind about what I really wanted in life and my purpose in life. The "Big 5 Personality Traits" listed below come from the article, "Personality Traits" (excellent by the way!) written by Edward Diener and Richard E. Lucas. The added information for each trait is my own.

My Personality TRAITS? Section 1

Take a personality test, identify traits associated with your personality and your personality type. Most tests consist of the basis to understanding them:

1. O for openness. Was I open to learning something new and enhancing what I already knew? Yes or No
   Why or Why not? _____
   _____

2. C for conscientiousness. Was I able to keep appointments, follow rules be hardworking? Yes or No
   Why or Why not? _____
   _____

3. E for extraversion. Am I sociable, talkative and engage in conversation with others? Yes or No
   Why or Why not?_____
   _____

4. A for agreeableness. Am I able to agree with other people, or work along with others? Yes or No
   Why or Why not? _____
   _____

5. N for neuroticism. Do I always have negative emotions like anger or worry all the time or most of the time? Yes or No
   Why or Why not? _____
   _____

Although I had many hobbies, or things I like to do. There were some things that I did almost every day, like reading or writing poems or poetry, collecting stamps/baseball cards. The Merriam-Webster Dictionary defines hobby as, **"A pursuit outside one's regular occupation engaged in especially for relaxation."**

My Hobbies? What do I like to do? How do I spend my time? Section 2

1. **I spend most of my time working five days a week.**
   a. Always.
   b. Sometimes.
   c. Rarely.
   d. I do not work.

2. **After work, I think about taking time to pursue one or more hobbies.**
   a. Always.
   b. Sometimes.
   c. Rarely.
   d. I do not have a hobby.

3. **On the weekends (Saturday and Sunday), I take time to relax with friends or at social events that have to do with different types of hobbies.**
   a. Always.
   b. Sometimes.
   c. Rarely.
   d. I work most weekends.

4. **I have one or more hobbies that I engage in at least once a month.**
   a. Always.
   b. Sometimes.
   c. Rarely.
   d. I work extra hours once a month.

5. **I spend money on or budget money for at least one hobby.**
   a. Always.
   b. Sometimes.
   c. Rarely.
   d. I spend money on necessities only or I do not have a budget.

My Hobbies? What do I like to do? How do I spend my time? Section 2 - continued

All-A's You balance your single parent lifestyle well with your work week and make time to engage with one or more hobbies that you enjoy.

All-B's You are on your way to achieving a balance between your single parent lifestyle and one or more hobbies that you enjoy.

All-C's You should find time to first relax in your single parent lifestyle and think about locating a hobby that you enjoy.

All-D's Consider taking some time in your single parent lifestyle to think about starting a hobby.

My Thoughts:

_____

_____

_____

_____

_____

_____

_____

_____

Money is important. It is a tool by which we use to obtain goods and services as well as conduct the lives that we live. As a single parent, money is a challenge to obtain and a challenge to hold on to because it's always channeled in one direction or another, to the babysitter or music lessons, or the rent/mortgage.

Money, Money, Money – Section 3

1. **How much money do you make each year working a job?**
   A. $20,000 or less.
   B. $30,000 - $40,000.
   C. $50,000 - $60,000.
   D. More than $60,000.

2. **How do I spend my money?**
   A. Household expenses, children (family), necessities.
   B. Luxury items, frivolous purchases, friends.
   C. Video games, music, online shopping.
   D. I save as much money as possible; I spend little.

3. **I live by a budget every month.**
   A. Always.
   B. Sometimes.
   C. Rarely.
   D. I do not have a budget.

4. **I have a checking or savings account with a local bank or credit union that I use regularly.**
   A. Always.
   B. Sometimes.
   C. Rarely.
   D. I do not have an account with a local bank or credit union.

5. **I give at least 10% of my salary each month to a charity, a church, or a foundation.**
   A. Always.
   B. Sometimes.
   C. Rarely.
   D. I do not give 10% of my salary.

<u>Money, Money, Money – Section 3 continued</u>

4 A's – As a single parent, you understand how much money you make and where it is spent each month. You managed to get money into a savings account.

4 B's – As a single parent, you understand how much money you make but you are working to obtain a balance in spending. Consider seeking a financial advisor or take a free budgeting course to maintain your money lifestyle.

4 C's – As a single parent, you understand how much money you make and gaining the balance of responsibilities, necessities and money management should be considered.

4 D's – As a single parent, you understand how much money you make but have other priorities that intervene with obtaining a good balance for your lifestyle.

Question 1A not included in answer section criteria.

My Thoughts:

_____
_____
_____
_____
_____
_____
_____
_____
_____

For a single parent, inspiration is just as important as money, I believe. Inspiration provides the power and the energy to face challenges, obstacles, and heartaches. If you have faith (unseen, internal connection of what is possible) in the journey of rearing and raising a family alone, one can overcome the challenges, obstacles and heartaches and keep living.

Inspiration - Have faith to believe! Section 4

1. **Do you believe that God gives us the faith to live on (through challenges, obstacles, heartaches) in life?**
   A. Yes.
   B. No.
   C. Maybe.
   D. I do not believe in God.

2. **Do you believe that we have the human strength to live on (through challenges, obstacles, heartaches) in life?**
   A. Yes.
   B. No.
   C. Maybe.
   D. I do not believe in human strength.

3. **Do you believe that inspiration in either of the ways listed is effective?**
   A. Prayer.
   B. Meditation.
   C. Positive affirmations.
   D. I do not believe either way is effective.

4. **How often do you pray, meditate, or recite positive affirmations?**
   A. Once a day.
   B. Once a week.
   C. Once a month.
   D. I do not pray, meditate, or recite positive affirmations.

5. **Music can also be a form of inspiration. Which genre of music helps to inspire and uplift you.**
   A. Gospel/Worship
   B. Rap
   C. Country/Swing
   D. R&B/Contemporary

Inspiration - Have faith to believe! Section 4 – Continued

4 A's – Your source of inspiration is consistent throughout being a single parent. It contributes to your well being and balance as a person and as a parent.

4 B's – Your source of inspiration is important to you as a single parent. However, consider what the source contributes to your well being and balance as a person and as a parent.

5 C's – Your source of inspiration is not that important to in being a single parent. Your well being and balance as a person and a parent is good enough.

5 D's - Your source of inspiration is not important to you as a single parent. Your well being and balance as a person and a parent is not important.

My Thoughts:

_____

_____

_____

_____

_____

_____

_____

_____

Diener, E. & Lucas, R.E. (2021). Personality traits. In R. Biswas-Diener & E. Diener (Eds), *Noba textbook series*: *Psychology*. Champaign, IL: DEF publishers. Retrieved from http://noba.to/96u8ecgw

About the Author

Zandra J. Deorosan is a native of the State of California. Born and raised in Sacramento, she attended Cosumnes River College in Elk Grove, CA where she found her love for writing and all things literary works. She especially loves children's books and creative writing which contributed to her niche for novels. Zandra studied Business at University of Phoenix where she obtained a Bachelor of Business Science Management and she studied Special Education at Grand Canyon University where she obtained a Master's in Education. Zandra began writing her debut book, Parent Power, after attending a parent and children conference. She discussed and provided commentary on parenting and raising and educating children. When she is not writing, she can be found listening to various genres of music and her favorites of contemporary gospel music, gospel rap music, and gospel jazz instrumentals. Zandra has begun writing her first children's book and currently resides in Atlanta, GA.

Printed in the United States
by Baker & Taylor Publisher Services